THE HARBOUR
WITHIN

A Book of Simple Spirituality

First published in 2016 by Hachette Books Ireland

A CIP catalogue record for this title is available from the British Library

Accounts of Sister Consilio's life were adapted from
A Haven of Hope: The Life and Work of Sister Consilio by Nora McNamara.
The author and publisher would like to acknowledge the use of this book with thanks.

ISBN: 978-1-4736-5024-4

Book design and typesetting: Anú Design, Tara
Printed and bound by Clays Ltd, St Ives PLC

Hachette Books Ireland policy is to use papers that are natural,
renewable and recyclable products and made from wood grown in sustainable forests.
The logging and manufacturing processes are expected to conform to the
environmental regulations of the country of origin.

Hachette Books Ireland
8 Castlecourt Centre
Castleknock
Dublin 15, Ireland

A division of Hachette UK Ltd.
Carmelite House
50 Victoria Embankment
London EC4Y 0DZ

www.hachette.ie

THE HARBOUR
WITHIN

A Book of Simple Spirituality

SISTER CONSILIO

HACHETTE
BOOKS
IRELAND

Contents

Living at soul level

To carry you through

A seven-day programme to live from the soul

Thoughts from the Old Dairy

Prayers from the Old Dairy

About Sister Consilio

Sister Consilio Fitzgerald was born in 1937 in Brosna, County Kerry, Ireland, the fifth child of seven born.

She trained as a nurse and midwife prior to joining the Sisters of Mercy in Athy, County Kildare, in 1959.

While working in St Vincent's Hospital, Sister Consilio came into contact with, and befriended, many 'road men' – men who had no home. From this came her idea for Cuan Mhuire ('The Harbour of Mary'), a place where these people could have a home, and a place where addictions could be treated.

In 2016 Cuan Mhuire celebrated its golden jubilee. In the fifty years of its existence Cuan Mhuire has helped more than 70,000 residents and has become Ireland's largest provider of addiction treatment, rehabilitation and step-down facilities. It now has five treatment centres (including one in Northern Ireland) and six transition house.

Sister Consilio's work for persons in addiction and

their families has been acknowledged by the President of Ireland, and in Great Britain her work has been recognised by the award of an honorary MBE from the Queen.

This is Sister Consilio's first book.

Note from the author

My hope for this book is that anyone searching for something, or looking for a sense of peace and happiness in their lives, will discover this harbour within by recognising themselves as the beautiful people they were created to be.

This book contains my thoughts on the value of recognising our own unique beauty and goodness, seeing the importance of love, family, friendship and prayer and the value of bringing God and Our Lady into our lives. This learning is a life journey which I'm still on. Life puts it up to me every single day, challenging me to work on my inner self and live from a soul level as I struggle with my human limitations. It's down to each of us to change ourselves to become what we can be and what God created us to be. There is so much help and support there to guide us through life. I hope that this book will

be a starting point for those who have forgotten how special and amazing they are or those who have yet to discover their own uniqueness and value in the world.

God Bless,
Sister Consilio

Prologue: The 'road men'

I wasn't long in St Vincent's Hospital in Athy, after I had been professed as a Sister of Mercy, when I first came across the 'road men'. I used to see them going from county home to county home with a bottle of wine in their pocket, sometimes staying in the little house down at the bottom of the garden at the hospital. They had left home and many had changed their names. They were homeless. They would often come to the hospital for some food. They had no purpose in their lives.

I imagined many of them came from farming backgrounds, each with their own sad story behind them of feeling rejected and rejecting themselves. They had no hope and were so ashamed of their lifestyles. I often talked to them and encouraged them to write home, especially to their mothers if they were still alive. They could not see that they were beautiful, gentle, good people who had unlimited capacity for kindness and generosity.

I realised that, along with shelter and food, they needed someone to show them compassion and love –

comforts that are taken for granted by so many of us. I would talk to them and listen as they poured out their troubles. I thought to myself that someday, somehow, I would have a place that these people could call 'home'. A place where they could go out to work from and could come home that night to a fire, a meal and someone to love them. I thought this would heal all of their woundedness. It took me quite some time to discover that the person they needed to love them was themselves – by this I mean they needed to be able to see their own goodness. To the present day I see that a lack of love and of being loved is at the root of all addiction.

In the beginning, I knew nothing about addiction. I was transferred from St Vincent's to work for a year in the convent kitchen. Shortly after that, the priest announced one Sunday morning that an open AA (Alcoholics Anonymous) meeting would be held in the hospital in Carlow. I got permission to go to the meeting with Sister Dominic the matron in St. Vincents and Sister Paschal. I had hoped that at a later stage Sister Dominic might allow me to do something for these people. During the meeting I borrowed a pen from Paddy – a publican from Athy who was sitting beside me. It was in fact Paddy who had organised that particular meeting.

A week later Paddy called to the convent to see me. I thought he was calling because I was interested in knowing more about addiction. He continued to call

once a week for a number of weeks. He then told me that his visits to the convent were helping him stay sober. After about six weeks he asked me to help Paddy D. who was in a bad state from drink. From then on many others started coming into the convent late and early, drunk and sober. This situation was causing problems in the convent and I asked Mother Sacred Heart if I could have the use of a small twelve-foot by eight-foot music room known as The Library. There was an outside door leading from it to the street, which was convenient. From then on we used that room, particularly at night time. A local electrician put in a plug and I bought a kettle and cups to the value of ten pounds. These were paid for when my sister, Sr Agnes, managed to get three matching cards from Surf washing-powder boxes and won a prize of ten pounds which she gave me. We used that little room for two years.

I used to bake an apple tart to have something to offer the visitors, who often came very late and stayed for a long time. They dreaded the long lonely nights. To my amazement, many began to get sober just through sharing their stories and through the fellowship and friendship that came of it in that tiny little room.

As word of the new haven spread, we began to run out of space and by the time winter came in 1966, we needed something bigger, as men and women from across the country came to us. The Old Dairy was located across

the yard from the convent kitchen and was used to store milk and butter. I began to think that it could well serve as a place where our visitors could come to be heard and listened to. I talked to Sister Patricia, one of the sisters in the kitchen, about how much easier it would be to have a fridge in the kitchen rather than running back and forth across the yard. She agreed and so I went to Mother Therese, the bursar, and it was agreed that I could have use of the Dairy in exchange for a refrigerator capable of holding the perishable food previously held in the Dairy. A few days later I saw an advertisement in the newspaper for a second-hand fridge for forty pounds. It was a huge amount of money at that time, but I rang the man who was selling it. I told him that we had no money but that he would be paid in due course. He said to come and get it. We set off for Waterford and took the fridge back to Athy on the roof of a car belonging to Tom H., a man who had also come looking for help. And in due course the man got his forty pounds. We cleared out the Old Dairy with the help of some of the men who had been coming to St Vincent's and who were now in recovery. This was the real start of Cuan Mhuire, a place built upon the goodness, kindness and talent of the people it helped.

And, looking back, I see even more clearly now that without the quiet support of a number of outstandingly good people who were prepared to trust me with the

work that was beginning to unfold, there might not have been any Cuan Mhuire. I'm thinking especially of Mother Sacred Heart, who was prepared to trust me and to go with the work – even though she knew I was very uncertain about it myself, she still supported me. There are some individuals who are gifted with *doing* things, and some who are graced with the wisdom to *affirm others* in what they are trying to do; she was one of the latter. Years later, Sister Sebastian reached out and anchored me when the road ahead was so uncertain. The trust and support of these great women, together with Cardinal Tomás Ó Fiach and Bishop Kavanagh, affirmed me and convinced me that Cuan Mhuire was meant to be and that it was my calling.

After some years, even though we had expanded somewhat, we knew that we would need a bigger place. One day, I saw an advertisement for forty-nine acres of land just outside the town of Athy. It was November 1972. Mother Sacred Heart reluctantly gave me permission to attend the auction even though she said that nuns didn't go to auctions. I went with a friend from the Dairy, Christy C. I still remember standing on the roadside as Christy bid for the farm. We came away having purchased the land for £49,000 which was a massive amount of money in those days. I didn't know where or how we would get the money to pay for the property. I trusted Our Lady as I did in all things. It was an act of faith.

The following morning, Mother Sacred Heart sent me on a message to the local bank. Unfortunately, the week before the auction, I had mentioned to the bank manager that we were hoping to buy the farm and on that occasion he asked me where did I expect to find the money. I replied, 'If God wants us to get it, then we will get it.'

He replied, 'We'll all start believing in God then, won't we?'

On this day, when I was doing the errand for Mother Sacred Heart, I had scarcely arrived inside the bank when the bank manager and his assistant appeared behind the counter. They both put out their hands and congratulated me on buying the farm. The manager then said to me, 'I want to see you inside.'

I replied (even though I didn't really mean it), 'I want to see you too, sir.'

He sat me down at the desk and said, 'I didn't sleep a wink all night worrying what would happen when a cheque would come in and there would be nothing to meet it.'

I said, 'I was thinking about you too, last night, but do you know what I was thinking? That you don't trust me.' I said I understood his responsibilities and his accountability for lending money. For his sake and for mine, I would have to go and find a bank manager, whoever that might be, who would trust me, because Cuan Mhuire would

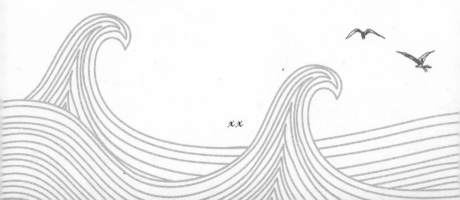

always be 'up and down' in any bank. He then reached his hand across the desk and, shaking my hand, he said to me, 'I trust you.'

The man who sold us the farm was quite ill and gave us permission to move in straight away. He died about a week later. It took a whole year for probate to come through, however, and this allowed us time to find the money.

In the meantime, we decided to build the first Cuan Mhuire on the land and we got two years' credit from the builders' providers. We applied to the County Council for planning. We were so stuck for space that we went ahead with the plans and the building was up by the time the planning came through. I asked the solicitor not to bother looking for money for the land from me until the last minute, because I wouldn't have any. He contacted me on a Friday and said I would have to have the money by twelve o'clock the following Monday.

I only had the Saturday to find money for the farm. By two o'clock on Saturday I had failed hopelessly to get any money, and I knew I had to have it by Monday. I went in to the games room in the new building and told our own people the story. They said, 'We'll pray to Our Lady.' A short while after we finished the prayers, a man walked through the door and said, 'I heard you're looking for a loan.' He said, 'Come to Dublin with me on Monday morning and we'll have it for you.' Our

Lady answered our prayers. This is just one of the many times she came to our aid. I could fill a book with all that Our Lady has done. That is why I always insist that what happens at Cuan Mhuire is Our Blessed Lady's work. The continuation of Cuan Mhuire as a community that enjoys and is appreciative of Her special friendship and protection very much rests on this conviction.

In those first years, I struggled with so much uncertainty in my own mind and so much opposition from all sides that I wondered whether I should continue with Cuan Mhuire or not. I found myself constantly asking: 'Am I right?' and 'Am I doing the right thing?'

In the back of my head I think I always knew that I was to go into religious life. In my final year of school, all I knew was that I didn't want to work in an office and I didn't want to be a dressmaker. I didn't like sewing at all.

After I had completed my Leaving Certificate, my father suggested that I might spend a year at home with my mother and himself, saying that they would be delighted with the prospect of having me around the home for another year as they might not have the opportunity of spending such a period of time with me

again. It was one of the happiest years of my life. My parents were extraordinary people. They gave us a lot of freedom and responsibility, and above all they showed us trust and love – unconditional love. It was great waking up in the morning without a care in the world, feeling the sheer joy of being there to assist my mother, who worked so hard, and to help my father around the farm. I used to love to walk with him through the fields and meadows.

At the time, my older sister Ita (Sister Agnes) was a member of the Sisters of Mercy in Ardee, County Louth. On one occasion when I paid her a visit, she suggested that I should start thinking about my future as my year at home would soon be up.

I was in two minds between training as a domestic-science teacher or training as a nurse. When I asked my father for his advice, he said, 'You should make up your own mind, but I think you know enough about cooking and housekeeping. If you went into nursing you could be of some use to someone.' I took his advice, and before I joined the Sisters of Mercy, I trained as a nurse in the North Infirmary Hospital in Cork, which was run by the Daughters of Charity. As part of the training we used to visit the sick and needy in Gurranabraher, a local Cork housing estate, and I spent a lot of my free time in Gurranabraher and got to know a lot of the good people who lived there.

Later I would find myself back in Gurranabraher when I was doing midwifery in St Finbarr's Hospital. While I was training, and indeed throughout my whole life, I knew that I was going to become a nun. It wasn't an idea I relished, as I wanted what most people want at that stage of their lives – marriage and a family of my own – but I knew it was what I was called to do. I still wanted to be able to see my family when they needed me and so I wanted to join an order that would allow me do that. Once I had finished my nurse's training, I heard of the Convent of Mercy in Athy and the great work that Sr Dominic, the matron in St Vincent's Hospital, was doing there. That decided it for me.

And so on 8 September 1959 I took the train from Mallow on my own. I felt my heart would break with loneliness getting on that train, saying goodbye to my brother Johnny at the station. I didn't know if I would survive it, but once I got to Athy, I knew that that was where I was meant to be.

It was hard going at times. That first year was my Spiritual Year and I found the structure and discipline hard after the freedom of my childhood.

During my second year in Athy, I also taught in the primary school. I loved working with children. After that year I began working in St Vincent's Hospital under Sister Dominic. It was in St Vincent's that I would first encounter the men and women who were to change my

life. I have learnt so much from these people, lessons that I now share with you in this book.

Living
at soul level

The harbour within

Every human being on this earth has unlimited capacity for goodness, gentleness, kindness, generosity, endurance, happiness and joy.

As we move through life, with its difficulties and worries and pressures, however, we begin to forget that we were all born with this uniqueness and goodness. We move away from the unconditional love of God with which we were born and we start to live more in our heads: we react with our mind to the challenges life presents to us. We let the ups and downs of life and its worries chip away at our self-belief. This takes us further away from God and unconditional love, and from being able to see the true goodness within ourselves and others.

We need to live more at a soul level because this is where God lives. Only in this way can we truly find peace and happiness in ourselves and in our lives.

When people begin to live at soul level, they discover the safe harbour that lies within each of us – a place to go to when life gets too stressful and worries too great. This safe harbour within is our sense of self, of being at peace with ourselves. It is made possible by knowing who we really are and where we come from and through love for ourselves and others, and it is essential to deal with what life throws at us.

This safe harbour is within each of us: we just need to find our way there.

Loving without any expectation

The most important thing in the whole wide world is love, and love is about seeing what's best in ourselves and in others.

To understand unconditional love we need to understand what it truly means to be a human being. We all have a body and a soul. At any given time we each have a choice whether to live at 'head level' or at 'soul level'. At 'head level', we are limited. We analyse everything, and our past experiences, our expectations of people, influence how we feel and how we react to situations. At a mental level we can feel let down by people and their actions. When we live at 'soul level', we have no expectations, good or bad, of people. We are therefore capable of unconditional love.

In fact, we are only capable of unconditional love at a soul level. Our heads are always expecting something in return. When we experience joy and happiness and create a positive energy around us, wherever we are or whatever we're doing, even in the middle of sufferings, the deep peace that we feel is coming from our souls.

This is unconditional love of ourselves, and it is hard to achieve, but this is the nature of God's love for us. It is also how we are *called* to love God and those around us.

My mother always showed deep kindness to the neighbours and those who might have had less than we did. I scarcely went home from school of an evening that she didn't hand me a bag with homemade bread, a bottle of milk or very often a clean shirt to bring to a neighbour. She would say, 'Run away with this and don't let anyone see you.'

I remember coming home from school one evening, climbing up on a chair to get to the press where I had hidden a new doll which I'd been given as a present a few weeks previously. My mother called from the kitchen,

'Are you looking for something?' and I said, 'No.' 'Well,' she said, 'if you're looking for the doll, I gave it to a little girl who called here today. You've had that doll for weeks and she has never had any.' I remember getting down off the chair disappointed, but I remember thinking that my mother loved me very much, but she also loved that little girl. It was a lesson I never forgot.

Years later when Cuan Mhuire came in to being, I used to think how would my mother feel if she saw one of her sons going from county home to county home with a bottle of wine in his pocket. Then I realised that she would see the men as her sons. At times when I brought them home with me, she and my father welcomed them as their very own.

The infinite value of God's gift to us

We are made in the image and likeness of God. When we die, our death notices speak of the 'remains'. What this actually acknowledges is that the part of us that is of infinite value has returned to God, and our bodies are what remain. What's most important is that we acknowledge that we have an eternal dimension to our lives and to our daily living. Not to acknowledge this reality is to live at a limited, human level. But to experience this is to acknowledge the eternal dimension of our lives.

We need to encourage people above all to see their own goodness, so that they can experience at a soul level this eternal power of God within themselves. It's in the most trying and difficult situations of our lives that we most need to go to our souls to reach our inner, deeper, better selves. This is where we find the power of God within us, and it is this eternal power that will always get us through the most demanding situations.

Your beautiful self

You will never meet anyone else like yourself. In all the billions of people created, no two are the same. That is amazing. Each one of us was created uniquely and yet God made each one of us in his image and likeness: what more could anyone want? He gave us this wonderful gift and the talent to make something of our own unique gift, even if we don't realise it yet. Many people are still searching for their talent. There is so much that people can do to find it, and so many ways that people can help others to find their own talent. It can be big or small, simple or complicated. What matters is that talent does exist within each of us; we just need to ask for help in finding it and using it. Once we ask for help, our prayers will be answered.

I am good. I was always good. God made me good.

I ask people I meet to say this to themselves one hundred times a day. So many people have never learnt this. Somewhere along the way we start to believe that we're not good enough. It might have just been a small thing, like being compared with another child. We lose faith in our own goodness. For many it's ingrained in their subconscious that they are not good enough. This idea that they are not good enough needs to be pushed out. Everyone was born good, and it's from this goodness that love grows.

You are unique and precious

Very often, people want to be like someone else. Over the years, I have visited many schools to talk to students. It's one of the things that I love doing, simply because the teachers and the students themselves are a joy to be with. Sometimes, you get the sense that students feel under pressure to compete with their peers. I talk to them about their *own* individual uniqueness and how special each one of them is, how they have been created special.

Sometimes they cry when they hear this. They don't hear it often enough. Each of us is fitted out by God with the talents we are meant to have and to use. Young people are under enormous pressure from the media and social networks to conform to this or that fashion and to compete with each other. This is so misguided. The most important thing you can do is to be your own beautiful self, as God created you. He never intended you to be like anybody else.

Our lives are so busy that our young people have nobody to help them discover their own special talent. Part of the education system should be to help each and every student to discover their own unique giftedness, so that they don't feel under pressure to compare themselves to others or to compete with others. So, we are equal in the sight of God – every one of us – but we are not all the same. Every one of us is unique with our own special needs and gifts.

This will help them to grow into adulthood knowing that they are special and unique, and this is a great help to becoming mature.

It's not about being better than the *next* person. *It's about finding and loving your own unique gifts and talents.*

And besides, as we get older, it becomes clearer to us how we can do nothing ourselves – but with God all things are possible.

There was never anyone made like you – and there never will be – not in all eternity. And that is a wonderful reality. It shows how special we are, that God has planned us so uniquely.

Be attentive to the present moment

Many people live in a constant state of restlessness, all the time striving to achieve more, have more, own more. For what? There is no security in this constant state of motion. We are tempted to worry about the future. Of course, it's natural to want to achieve more in your job and to want to be comfortable and secure financially. But it's when these desires get in the way of our happiness that they begin to cause real problems. The only time we have to be happy is *now*. God gives us the present moment so that we can be fully attentive to all of the graces, the power to do things, that are embedded in the present moment and so that, being attentive, we can begin to use our God-given talents at any moment – like *now*.

As children we grew up picking potatoes on the farm, and you'd be doing it all day long. You could only concentrate on where you were. All manner of work that we do with our hands can provide a great opportunity for attentiveness. It could be polishing a table or chopping vegetables. Plasterers, for example, have to focus on one place at a time and on each trowel as they go. This is how we need to approach everything we do. When we do, it leads to great calm and peace. Attentiveness is always at soul level. Remember, we don't have to believe it. It's necessary only to practise it and we can then actually experience it: the power of God within us.

. . . . .

'A man will walk more in a day than he'll run'

. . . . .

Pace yourself. Be attentive.

Keep things simple

My father was a man possessed of a great sense of humour, a hearty laugh and a twinkle in his eye. He had a particular fondness for the simple pleasures in life: sitting by the blazing hearth fire at night time and entertaining everyone with stories, jokes and poetry. He loved the land, which had been tilled by my mother's family for generations. Every shrub, every tree, every blade of grass was precious in his sight. He believed that the task at hand was the most important task, and approached everything he did in that way – from picking potatoes to clean-raking the meadows to the turf that was cut and laid sod by sod on the bank.

There couldn't be a more ordinary or plain country person than I am. I never went beyond it. I'm very aware that God created us all equal – it's not as if some of us are up there and some down here.

My living is very simple – I believe in keeping everything as simple as possible. I'm drawn to the most simple things – it's like the Old Dairy where we started Cuan Mhuire. It was so simple. When you are a part of something and you are loved you need nothing more. My life is very simple – it's clear to me that by myself I can do nothing, but with God all things are possible.

Keep life simple – and the simplest thing of all is handing it over to God.

Surrender to God's plan

In the early days, I struggled with uncertainty: was God really calling me to Cuan Mhuire to do this work? There was so much opposition from all sides that I was constantly asking myself whether I was doing the right thing. I had prayers that brought me great comfort and brought me through all of the ups and downs of those days – and especially through those long nights. There were times when I said some of the prayers in this book, even though I could very well be up all night with somebody in distress, but I kept saying them, and they eased my fears and worries.

I found myself in a situation with the Old Dairy where there was opposition to the centre coming from every side. At the same time, there were very sick people coming from all over the country because they had nowhere else to go except a locked ward in a psychiatric

hospital. I had to turn to God. And God helps in so many ways, including sending people to help. We wouldn't have been able to open without the support of a doctor and I was fortunate enough to have a local doctor on board, Des O'Neill. His courage and commitment to helping his fellow man, as well his sense of humour, were just extraordinary. Turning to the Lord Himself and His Mother, I had a prayer which I wrote out, placed on the wall and said over and over again, every day:

· · · · ·

Jesus, I surrender myself to you, take care of everything.

· · · · ·

Even though I might not have meant it or believed it all the time, I still said this prayer, and it brought me through fire and water. And I'm here to tell the tale. Fifty years down the line, I find myself saying it over and over again, every day, because I know now how foolish it is not to trust in God, who knows what is best for us and who loves us with a love beyond all telling.

All of us are equal

God created us equal. It doesn't matter who we are or what we are about: we are all equal in the eyes of God. We are all *loved* equally by God, and we are all worthy of respect and dignity.

But remember – we are also unique – unlike any other person – special to God.

In Cuan Mhuire, when we see someone coming through the door, we see in the face of that person the face of Jesus Christ himself. Remember what He said to us: '*as long as you did this for the least of my brothers, you did it for me.*'

This is the belief that enables us to look beyond appearances, beyond behaviours and beyond likes and dislikes – and see the Lord. This is the reality that enabled me to keep going when the going was tough. It is so easy to lose sight of this. Seeing Christ in all who

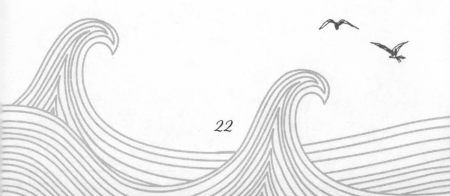

came to us and all who work with us is the true mark of God. Sometimes we can miss this and we have to pick ourselves up and start over again.

Use your talents

We don't have to be the best at everything. We don't have to have loads of talent: we just need to find and use what we have been given by God. If we can do that as best we can, we will live fulfilled lives. It's not about being the best or the most successful: it's about doing as much as we can with what we have. If we do what's possible with the little we have, it will grow and grow. We should not compare ourselves to others. You can do great things with the talents you were born with: simple things which will help others and which will make those around you happy and that will bring its own reward. We all have different talents. Mossie, my brother and eldest sibling, worked so hard around the farm to help my father and for me, Mossie and home were synonymous. He works very hard. His family, that he brought up so well, play a major part in the work of Cuan Mhuire. My brother Johnny had a rare gift for building. When we were all

little, my mother used to say that my brother Johnny and I were like twins. Johnny and I had a great bond from the very start. He was always around through my childhood and when I began Cuan Mhuire Johnny gave us the generous gift of his talents. Our centres at Athy, Bruree, Newry, Cork, and indeed other facilities, were the product of his hard work. They are a lasting legacy of all he did for Cuan Mhuire over the years – and he did it so quietly.

My brother Joe has always been so special to me. He had the gift of making me feel safe. As a young child I waited for him after school so I could go home with him. Joe has always been a very reflective, wise and gentle person. Joe has worked hard, and quietly, and has supported me throughout the years.

My sister Ita – better known as Sister Agnes – joined the Sisters of Mercy before me. I could not tell you how

much she and her talents and abilities have brought to Cuan Mhuire. How she has supported me and everyone in Cuan Mhuire down the years. Sister Agnes has transformed many lives.

I see so many people with talent who get caught up in thinking too much and become paralysed. What prevents people from taking action might well be something that happened them earlier in life, something that lingers in the back of their minds. I remember in school being told that I wasn't good at composition. In fact, I had misunderstood an exercise the teacher had asked me to do and I got slapped. And after that I always hated writing letters. It took me nearly sixty years to understand why I always put off writing letters. But I'm no better or worse than the person standing beside me. What does it matter? Now I just write the letter and send it off.

Appreciate those around you

My mother and father unquestioningly supported all my decisions through the years. My mother was seventy when I opened the first Cuan Mhuire and supported me for the remaining nineteen years of her life.

In November 1983, I had returned home from Athy, as my mother was dying. My father was also bedridden at the time, but before she died, my mother beckoned him to her bedside. She whispered in his ear that she had forgotten to tell him earlier that if she was starting her life all over again, he would be the man that she would marry. My mother passed away a few days later on 6 November 1983 aged eighty-nine and my father just eleven months later when he was eighty-four on 7 October 1984.

My parents had a long and sometimes difficult life together. But the one constant in our family and our childhood was the love our parents showed to each other,

to their children and to others. It wasn't always easy – nothing worthwhile ever is.

Parenting today can be very difficult. There are so many aspects of life jutting in to compete for your time, whereas years ago you sat down by the fire and had time to be present with your children. Listening is the most important thing, and saying 'I love you' and 'you are important'.

But the love between a child and a parent can also be complicated, and it requires work and effort. It is hard for parents to know what to do for their children when they are in distress, as no two children are the same, but all children should be accepted and enjoyed exactly as they are.

It's twelve or thirteen years since I was working in the Drugs Unit in Athy, and I got on great with the young lads there. I always thought they saw me as their grandmother, and that, in this way, they felt more easily accepted by me. Grandparents need to tell their grandchildren how good they are; sometimes such positive reinforcement can be easier for a child to hear from a grandparent than from their own parents. A child's relationship with a grandparent is simpler, as grandparents are under less pressure and have less responsibility. Grandparents may also have more time and life experience to share, and to help to meet the basic needs of a child, than young parents who are trying to make ends meet. A grandparent's time with their grandchildren is simply invaluable.

Neighbourly love

In the weeks following the birth of my youngest sister, Agnes, my mother needed a bit of help because she had her hands full with the new baby. I was three years of age at the time. For a full week, to give my mother a break, my father would lift me over the fence to our neighbour Peg Roche and place me gently in her arms each morning as he went off to work on the farm.

I'll always remember going down to our neighbour Lily's, too, and being lifted in to her bed. It felt special because at the time she had no children, and there were no other children around. There were so many neighbours who showed me – and my parents – so much love as a child and helped me to set out on life's journey believing that all people are good.

The importance of seeing the positive

Positivity is *always* more powerful than negativity, and that is why it's so important to emphasise goodness – particularly in young people.

While deep down I always knew that I was destined to become a nun, that day in 1959 when I entered the Sisters of Mercy in Athy, I felt my heart would break from loneliness. My brother Johnny took me to the railway station in Mallow. He could see how upset I was and tried to persuade me to return home with him. I reasoned that the nuns were waiting for me in Portlaoise. I figured that I would see at Christmas how I felt once I had satisfied my conscience. But once I entered the convent, I knew there was no other life for me.

One part of our training was a daily examination of conscience where we had to sit for twenty minutes and examine our failings. I never got very far with it. I found myself thinking about my failings and marking them down in a little black book. Then one day I thought, 'This is getting me nowhere.' I resolved there and then to leave my failings behind me and to focus on what is best in me. By doing this, we can create a capacity to seek out what is best in others.

The home within

Every human being has five basic needs which need to be met:

> We need to be heard.
> We need to be seen.
> We need to be accepted as we are.
> We need to be believed and to be believed in.
> We need to have a safe place.

Home is the safe place that we all need. That feeling of safety is created first by our parents and other significant people in our lives. However, if we don't receive this love, we might look for it elsewhere and sometimes through destructive behaviour. People who didn't receive this love when they were younger, or through life, can be wounded but it's important to realise that you will always be the beautiful, valuable person God created you

to be. Finding a home has to start first with remembering that you have a home within: God and Our Lady are always there for us, to help us on the road back to the safe harbour within.

To carry
you through

Have you ever been in a dark place and thought there was no hope, that there was nothing you could do and no one who could help?

There is always help to carry you through. There are things you can do to help yourself and there are people who can help. In this part of the book I will tell of some of the things that have helped to carry me and others through.

Above all, I would remind you that God and Our Lady are always there to help.

You just need to open your mind and your heart. When I opened our first centre, it was on the news. Back in those days TVs were very different and there was no pause or rewind buttons. Next time I went home, my father said, 'I saw you on the box, and I'm glad you didn't think you were doing it yourself,' meaning that I had benefitted from the help of God and Mary. This help is available to all of us in our times of trouble, worry or need.

Borrow someone else's faith

My mother had great faith, and I saw this in action when I was a young child when it came to my schooling.

I had no problems at school, but I was careless about homework. I didn't worry too much about it. I was always too busy helping my father in the fields or with the cows or running errands for my mother.

One morning when I was walking to school, I hadn't done my homework and knew that this could mean trouble. Then I thought about my mother, and about the 'Lady' who helped her when she was in difficulties, and how her prayers were answered. I decided to ask for Our Lady's help, which I got: the teacher never checked my homework that day! And from that day to this Our Lady has helped me every day of my life. I just couldn't imagine living life without Her help.

If you have difficulty in believing, borrow someone

else's faith, as I borrowed my mother's faith, and it won't be long until you find your own. It's there for the asking, but the change you will experience is real.

Jugs of positive energy

There can at times be so much negativity around us and it needs to be counteracted. The people who come into Cuan Mhuire are so down, as there is so much negativity attached to addiction. I think of what we do in those first few weeks as being like taking jugs of positive energy and pouring them over them continually without them knowing it.

I find this is a very powerful tool for life and I have taught so many people it over the years. Make a conscious choice to pour jugs of positive energy over yourself. And then you can share it with others during the day.

The gift of faith

The greatest gift that my parents gave to me was the gift of faith. Seeing their prayers being answered gave me the assurance that I wouldn't be travelling the journey of life on my own. Even when I was a very small child, when anything went wrong or I saw anything that upset me, it was a great comfort to know I could ask Our Lady or the Lord Himself for help, and that they would come to my aid. In this way, I never felt alone.

There is a saying: 'The family that prays together, stays together.' It is so true. It's the best investment of time that you will ever make in the life of your children. I would encourage you, and everyone, to find that time every evening to pray with your children. I have seen the power of prayer in families that have been through great difficulties. It brings the family together for 'time out' and time with each other – and that is a great thing, especially when there are so many distractions in life these days. When children see the example of their parents coming together and praying, it creates a very powerful impression on their young minds.

Be aware of your own goodness

If asked to list six bad things about themselves, many people have no trouble answering. But ask them to list just one good thing and they're stuck.

A lot of people I meet are not aware that they are good people. It's really very simple. We all have the capacity for goodness within us. It is important that we are aware of this goodness within each of us and in each other.

I encourage everyone to see their own goodness by giving it away to others in what they do and say. In this way, they can re-educate their subconscious and get rid of the lie that told them they are no good. Of course, all of this takes time. It cannot be done in a hurry – there are no shortcuts.

In the early days of the Old Dairy I was so busy that our residents had to learn to look out for one another. There were three public houses quite close by, and the temptation would always be there to visit them, but

everyone used to look out for each other and mind each other and this would stop people making wrong decisions. In this simple act of generosity, they saw that they were capable of goodness, of making a difference to someone else's life, which was hugely empowering and healing for everyone.

If we could only be aware of our own capacity for healing each other by focusing on the best within ourselves, and the best within others, we'd all be in a better place.

Make room in your soul

Meditation is never easy. It could be the most demanding activity of your whole day. Remaining silent for twenty minutes is challenging but it gives great calm.

Meditation is something we take on to do as an act of faith. When we meditate we are not asking for or expecting anything. We are simply allowing ourselves to be.

I like to meditate twice a day, twenty minutes in the morning and twenty minutes in the evening.

Meditation grounds me and helps me to let go of what is going on in my head. If I didn't meditate I know that my head would much more often be getting in the way of my heart.

Cutting meditation or prayer short because I'm busy is a disadvantage – it's no shortcut. Time spent in meditation or prayer is never wasted.

Friendships to carry us through

When I was going to secondary school in Abbeyfeale, I used to stay with my aunt and uncle, Mary and Bartholomew Guiney. They lived in Knocknasna, on a small farm outside Abbeyfeale. They had no children of their own and they lavished attention on me.

Later, when I was training to be a nurse, I would come back to Knocknasna on my holidays. When I did, some of the boys planned that a different one of them would see me home after the dances. I wasn't aware of their plans. I met them and danced with all of them. I hadn't the heart to put any one of them in front of the other, so I suggested we all do the walk together. All these boys have remained my good friends throughout my life. Perhaps in those days life was simpler; relationships were more life-giving, beautiful and lasting.

In times of stress we need to have friendship to pull us through. Friendship is so important. I've been blessed

with so many good friends in my life. It's just as important to be a friend to someone: to be there for them. When my mother died so many people came up to me to say, 'Your mother was a very special friend to me.'

Without friendship and really true friends who were always there to support and help in the many and varied difficult times, it would be impossible to carry through with all the demands Cuan Mhuire made on all of us in the early days. Very often late at night, at two or three o'clock, when every resident was settled down for the night, we would gather around the cooker for a cup of tea before going to bed. When all was quiet and hushed we would chat and laugh together about the many ups and downs of the day. We lightened each other's burdens with our sharing, light-heartedness and support. These friends I can never forget. I trust that many of them are gone to heaven. Those who are still alive are truly precious. They carried Cuan Mhuire on their shoulders and have left their mark.

We need to love and cherish these people we meet who become true friends as much as we can. And we need to allow ourselves to be cherished.

Walk in another's shoes

When we feel slighted or are holding a grudge against someone, it is helpful to go through events and consider that they may have been going through some pain themselves. We all need to learn to walk in another's shoes, to think about what might be going on in their lives. This is a habit we can all learn, and it is a great thing to encourage children to do. When we do this there is no room for selfishness, greed and jealousy that can so easily undermine harmony. The more we give our best to others, and the more we see the best in others, the more healing takes place and the power of love will work wonders.

The gift of tough times

We all suffer at times. No one's life is all plain sailing, and I certainly have had tough times in my life. I have found the words of Saint Padre Pio – 'Suffering is a gift from God; blessed is he who knows how to profit from it' – a huge consolation to get me through difficult times.

If we are suffering, we should remember:

•••••

'He who learns must suffer. And even in our
sleep, pain that cannot forget falls drop by
drop upon the heart, and in our own despair,
against our will, comes wisdom to us by the
awful grace of God.'

– *Aeschylus*

•••••

We can remember that when we are suffering, even in the blackest hours, wisdom will surely come.

Depression

Depression is a terrible and at times a dangerous thing. However severe or otherwise it may be, it is undeniably a bad situation to be in.

People need help to work through depression. It can be something simple like going for a walk with someone or being attentive to your surroundings. Engaging with nature can be a great friend to people who are trapped in depression. In order to come out of your depression, you have to move beyond what you're thinking to being attentive to something you can do: rediscover the gifts you are so capable of using. There is no hurry and no pressure.

Very often, depression is congealed anger, hurt and pain. A depressed person might not even be aware of it, as it can be the result of pain from the past or suffering that wasn't dealt with or lived out. We have to live out the pain of the past, live through it and work it out until it is gone, but nobody wants to face in to that kind of

work, understandably enough. So, you have to give it time, which involves working through the pain of the past when you feel you can.

Living out and working through the hurt of the past is a slow and painful process, and can often be helped by a group setting for mindful discussion and quiet contemplation. Medication can play a role, but self-help support groups can help people to manage their pain in the long term. Being open to help is the key, because it's very difficult to come out of depression alone. It can be a great support to know that somebody is available to you, someone who puts no expectations on you. You might be blessed with family and friends you feel you can talk to, but if not, appeal to God and Our Lady. If I didn't know that there was someone I could call through my faith, I'd be lost. I don't know how people cope with what life throws at us without a belief that someone is there for us always, looking after us. Knowing that there is a greater power than ourselves can help.

Letting go of the past

If you are haunted and bound by negative aspects of your past that make you anxious or worried or prevent you from being free, then you need to forgive yourself. You will find great freedom in that.

Sometimes, we feel slighted and hurt by what other people do to us. We need to understand that, a lot of the time, the actions of others have nothing to do with us and everything to do with their own unhappiness. If we can remember that when someone next lashes out at us, we can learn to let go of such slights against us and not let them affect us. Try not to react with your mind to something someone says or does; take the time to step back and act directly from your soul.

Grieving

People have to give themselves time to grieve when they lose a loved one. If you have someone who can listen to you at such a time, you need to talk to them. When I was grieving for my brother Johnny, whom I was very close to, I stayed on his farm looking after the animals, crying my heart out. I had to give myself that time. A while later I was doing a course on coaching and grieving came up, and again I spent a day on that course crying. We have to cry out our pain, even when it comes to us in waves. It's a big part of healing. Be aware of your pain. Give yourself time and a place to grieve.

Illness

Being ill for a long time is a major cross, both for the ill person and for their family. People who are ill, of course, need a lot of support and help, and we should always reach out to them. Being confined to places is also a cross, as is the experience of being alone in a nursing home or hospital, and loneliness can be a greater suffering than a physical one.

Illness is part of our human condition. It's very tough, especially when there are children involved – be it children who are sick or children with family members who are also ill. Over the years, I have known people who have been through seas of sorrow and pain related to illness, and I've been ill, though not in a prolonged way. I hope and pray that I would have the grace to accept it if it comes my way.

All of us directly or indirectly have been touched by illness of one kind or another. Being ill can be redemptive too, because it can bring us closer to our faith. I was so very struck by how Pope Saint John Paul II endured his final years and months with such dignity, and how so many millions were touched by this. In our pilgrimage to Lourdes every year we see the great grace of healing, including acceptance, that is part and parcel of illness and human suffering.

Christ experienced an ocean of suffering, at every level. It is out of His understanding of suffering that Christ enjoined on us the importance of visiting the sick and those who are confined; it's part of what it means to be truly Christian.

A place I change myself, not anyone else

In the very early days of Cuan Mhuire I put a plaque on the wall saying 'Cuan Mhuire is a place where I can change myself, not anybody else'. I thought at the time that it would be wonderful if we all practised what was written on the plaque. I didn't realise at the time that I was preaching what I needed to learn the most.

I started trying to change people when I was quite young. I thought that if a couple of people changed and understood each other better we would have heaven on earth. I thought it was others who needed to change. I tried to make this happen but, of course, I didn't succeed in doing so. It was an impossible task.

This pattern stayed with me. I couldn't see it or I couldn't hear it from those who tried to tell me. Then, one day about ten years ago, I was at a meeting. I am not

sure what the meeting was about – possibly about self-awareness and self-acceptance – and it suddenly dawned on me what I had been doing.

As I realised this I felt great freedom. I decided to stop beating myself up about it. It got up and left me. It was such a relief. I was given the grace to let go of my addiction to wanting to change others. At the time one of the people I had wanted to change was still alive and I'm sure it was a great relief to him that I had given up this wish to change him.

This was a huge lesson to me. It opened my eyes to the blindness of addiction – all those years I had talked and written about addiction but I was blind to what was going on in me. I often think that I was lucky that it wasn't a substance I was addicted to because it took me so long to wake up to it – if I had been addicted to something other than changing others I'd most likely have died from it.

We all have our own addictions and it can be a long time before the penny drops and we see our blindness to ourselves; we can change no one else – only ourselves!

Our Lady's friendship

I have been asking Our Lady for help since I was a very young age and I trust I will continue to do so until my dying day. She has always answered my call for help. She has saved me from many tragedies and hardships and has guided me all the way. If I didn't have Our Lady, I sometimes doubt whether I would have the courage to keep going.

I know that I am never worthy of Our Lady's love, but the beautiful thing about Her is that She is not a fair-weather friend. She is not just there when you are doing the right thing. She is there when I mess things up. When the whole world seems to be going wrong, She comes in. I love Her deeply, though I wish I showed it more often. Everyone, regardless of their beliefs or religion, can find and experience the friendship and love of Our Lady. There are no friends like Her. She already loves you. She is always reaching out a hand to help you.

Today or in the future, you can allow Her to lead you to where you are meant to go and to become the beautiful person you were created to be.

Our Lady helps and protects us. Cuan Mhuire bought a place in Newry in 1984 at the height of the Northern Ireland Troubles. There was then no centre in Northern Ireland, and they were having to come down to us in the Republic. The health authority people came in and said 'do you realise that you're sitting on a bomb?' I said, 'Our Lady will take care of us.' We had people from the IRA, the UDA, the UVF, all organisations and denominations, yet I never saw a row among them. From both sides of the political divide I would hear all stories. They would tell me of the horrendous things they had experienced or sometimes done themselves. I always encouraged them to talk to Our Lady, who is a real mother to all of us; that they should all be grateful to Our Lady because it was down to Her that Cuan Mhuire existed. I'd tell them to be respectful to Our Lady in the same way they would be respectful to someone who gave Cuan Mhuire food or money. Many of the Protestant men and many who had no faith became more devoted to Our Lady than the Catholic ones. Our Lady is not about religion. She is about all of us just as we are.

In Cuan Mhuire we have always been protected by Our Blessed Lady. When we didn't have the price of something we needed – I knew Our Lady would help. She'll do for all people what She did at the wedding feast at Cana – She called Her son in to help, and She doesn't put any conditions on helping.

Guardian angel

Each of us has a guardian angel to take care of us. How privileged we are to have such protection. How often we take our guardian angel for granted. I've neglected my guardian angel but I know that he is always there for me. I have been more attentive in recent times. This may be out of necessity. I seem to be needing him more, as I am getting older. I ask my guardian angel to do things I can't get around to doing. If I can't get someone on the phone whom I urgently need to contact, I ask my guardian angel for help, which he never fails to give me.

I know I shouldn't just be using my angel to go here and there for me. They take their position very seriously: they are not airy-fairy beings. Angels are immensely powerful spiritual beings, and the presence of angels can be seen at every significant event in the life of Our Lord and of the Holy Family. The angel Gabriel didn't

equivocate when he came to speak to Our Lady. He said what he had to say.

When I was a child, a picture in school showing the guardian angel protecting two children as they crossed the brook really impressed me. It gave me a great sense of security and of being protected myself. The brook was familiar to me, as we crossed 'the footbridge' on our way to and from school every day.

The power of forgiveness

Forgiveness brings great peace. It draws out the goodness in both parties. But it can take time for us to understand the power of forgiveness – and to act on it. When I was younger, I thought forgiving people was no problem. I had no difficulty with forgiveness. When I ran into more difficult circumstances, I couldn't believe the difficulty I had in forgiving. I finally realised that the reason I had found it easy to forgive people in the past was because I had had nothing to forgive in the first place. And then later, when there was more at stake, I truly struggled with it, and I prayed. I didn't want to be in that situation. But it did give me a far better understanding of the many people I was meeting who were having such difficulties with forgiveness. I finally saw where these people were coming from.

After a couple of years of struggling, I went to a Healing Mass and Service in Clonfert, Co. Galway. On

my way back to Dublin, I just felt that all of my negativity about forgiveness had lifted from me. I'm so grateful it never came back again. This was a key learning experience for me, because lack of forgiveness is a major obstacle for many people.

As a result of my own experience, I understand first hand that getting to a point where you can forgive yourself or others is simply not possible to do on our own in many situations. I see it as a question of God's grace: when we find ourselves in such a situation, we have to ask for, pray and wait patiently for the grace to forgive.

Lack of forgiveness in anyone's life is a major block and the grace to forgive always brings a new-found freedom. Forgiveness brings freedom for ourselves and for whomever we found it difficult to forgive, because we also pray for them.

To forgive those around you, pray for the grace to do

so. You may need more help and the support of others too; for me, it was the Healing Mass and Service that made all the difference.

For many people, trouble with forgiveness can be transmitted across the generations of a family; it can be a learned behaviour that has to be addressed and resolved.

Forgiveness is a hugely important part of marriage and family life and is dependent on communication, something with which many people struggle. It's the lack of communication, and a lack of *awareness* of each other's pain, which can be a terrible obstacle to overcome and can even lead to a break down in the marriage. There is of course help available to couples in crisis. In my own experience of working with couples in difficulty, a helpful step can be for the husband and wife to be encouraged to focus on the difficulties of the *other* person and not on their own. Doing this takes people out of themselves and is a major step in the recovery of a marriage. Forgiveness becomes less complicated when we think about the other person. What's not acknowledged can't be forgiven. So it is important that each of them acknowledges their own particular vulnerability and that they have compassion for each other.

Breaking the jam jar

Sometimes, we need to let our emotions out. We shouldn't bottle things up, and if something is upsetting us mentally and emotionally we need to let it out. This is very important. Many different courses and books on doing our 'inner work' suggest that there are times when we need to relive the anger of our past in order to physically let it out – by breaking a jam jar or splitting a log of wood – and to release, in a non-destructive way, the anger that would otherwise congeal in us.

Like many, I remember a time when we didn't speak about depression; we didn't know too much about it. There was a man near Athy who used to get into terrible blackness and pain with depression. I asked his neighbour how he was, and he replied, 'He'll be better shortly. I saw him yesterday with his black overcoat out on the line, and he was flogging it.' The man was acting out his pain. His body knew what would help, even if his mind didn't.

The gift of Confession

The importance of being told that your sins are forgiven is huge. I see men and women coming out of Confession and you can see the relief and release on their faces. It's so important to know that, in the eyes of God, you are forgiven. Saint Padre Pio spent his whole life healing people from his confessional. It can be difficult to examine our own conscience. They say that the only people who like Confession are the very scrupulous! Many of us do not avail of the great graces given in Confession. We are not aware of what a great gift this sacrament is.

The Green Scapular

One expression of Our Lady's love for us all is the Green Scapular. I put a great faith in the Green Scapular. What really made me believe in it was that, in the year I started nursing, I was in the female surgical on a Sunday evening, and there was a young woman there who had been diagnosed with cancer of the glands. She was crying and worrying about her young children – what would they do when she died? At that time – the mid-fifties – there was no cure for cancer.

Sometimes I would see someone wrap the Green Scapular around a patient's wrist as they went down for surgery – these were the days before strict hygiene rules!

I remembered that I had read on a leaflet about the Green Scapulars, which were in a drawer in each ward in the North Infirmary, that a priest had been cured from cancer as a result of his faith in a Green Scapular he received from a nun. I went to a drawer, took out a

Green Scapular and we both said a prayer to Our Lady and the woman put the Green Scapular around her neck. Next morning she went for further tests and the results were all clear. The cancer had been treated.

Once in 2003, when I was in New York at an event, a man from Donegal walked up to me. He said that his father had been with me in the Old Dairy, and when he opened his hand, in it was his father's Green Scapular. It was the only thing he had kept of his father's. People don't have to believe in it themselves – they just need to put it somewhere close by them.

Note: For more information on the Green Scapular contact Green Scapular Guild, 339 S. Seton Ave., Emmitsburg, MD 21727. 301-447-6606. www.setonheritage.org

Lourdes

Lourdes is a most special place, graced by Our Lady's appearance to St Bernadette. It's a place where we are very much aware of her love of all who suffer. It's a place of great healing.

Years ago, nuns needed special permission from the bishop to go to Lourdes. It wasn't done, and going to Lourdes was the last thing that was on my mind – I didn't want another reason for people to say I was out of line!

But in the end, I went. Our Blessed Lady wanted me to go. Here's how it happened. Two members of Alcoholics Anonymous were going on the army's annual pilgrimage, and they decided on their way home from the Dairy one night that they were going to bring me. They rang the convent the next day and told me their intention but I said I wouldn't be granted permission. They asked me to speak to the Reverend Mother. I asked her, saying I didn't want to go anyway; she said I was

better off to say no. The next day Big Joe arrived and told Reverend Mother that he knew she couldn't give permission, but asked if she could ask Mother General about it. Mother Gabriel said she would ask the bishop, but more than likely, I could go. The permission was granted. It was decided I should travel to Lourdes.

So I went, and the very first night I was in Lourdes I heard a racket up and down the corridor of where we were staying in the Guest Women's Barracks. But because the army was so regulated, I didn't dare go and ask if they needed help. When I went down in the morning I met the chaplain and the matron, who were talking about the lady who broke out 'on the drink' the previous evening. They were making plans for her to go home. I asked if I could do anything – I was happy to help her. I knew very little about addiction at the time, as I was only just set up in the Dairy. But they were

happy to put her into my care, and I remained in her company throughout the pilgrimage. She came home with me, well and sober, and never drank again.

It was a sign for me. At the time, I was struggling. I wasn't sure what was the right thing to do. This was the sign that confirmed for me that staying with the infant Cuan Mhuire was what Our Lady wanted me to do.

I went back to Lourdes the following year with a group. There were four or five of us who went to Confession there, and they all went to one particular priest. I went to someone else. When they came out they told me that he could tell them all about their lives, and that I had missed out. So I went to see him, and told him I'd been to Confession already, but just wanted his blessing. He said to me that I had a lot of work to do in Lourdes and that I would be back many times. He went on to explain that I would go home and get sick, but not to worry, I

would get well. People would, he said, 'be talking' – but to pay no heed to it. He told me that things would work out. I've been back to Lourdes at least forty times since then.

In spite of not wanting to infringe the rules, Our Lady took me to Lourdes and confirmed through the meeting with the priest (who knew nothing of Cuan Mhuire or myself – who could have had no idea that I was a nun, because I was dressed as a nurse) what my work would be in the future.

Cuan Mhuire's year begins with our annual pilgrimage to Lourdes. Every year we bring new people there, and they find it life-giving, enlightening, healing. We always start our year when we get back from Lourdes feeling ready to begin anew.

Eat the frog

Dwelling on all kinds of negativity prevents our spiritual growth, and it takes all kinds of forms in our daily lives. Some people have trouble getting past 'Monday morning blues', but the trouble is mostly in our minds.

When I was in secondary school, I used to cycle in to the Convent of Mercy in Abbeyfeale. I got on my bike on a Monday morning at 6.30 a.m. so I could get in to school to catch up on the homework I had neglected to do at the weekend. The heavier the rain poured down on a Monday morning, the better I liked it. You see, if our clothes were wet in school, we were sent down to the boiler house to dry them – and this meant we escaped class. There were many Monday mornings when I thought I was not wet enough to escape class and on those occasions I would get off at a well at the top of a hill in Killconlea and dip my skirt in the water so I could

go to the boiler room. I didn't like facing school on a Monday morning, but once we got out at 3.30 p.m., I would say, 'The week is over!' – as I really didn't mind the rest of the week.

Years later, my good and wise friend Susan Dargan used a phrase that really gets across what we need to do on those Monday mornings: 'Eat the frog.' Get rid of the stuff you don't want to face – just do it. Do the thing that you dislike having to do. Embrace Monday morning – eat the frog! – and the rest of the week will take care of itself.

Practise gratitude every day

We live in a world full of entitlement, which can sometimes blind us to the power of gratitude. Without gratitude, there is no joy. All of us need to be grateful that we can get out of bed every day; we can be grateful for the gift of life every day.

When I worked in the Drug Unit in Athy, there were three lads in each room working to recover from addiction. When the knock on the door came to get up every morning, it was the responsibility of one of them to say out loud, 'Isn't it great to be alive?' And the other two would chorus back at him, 'Isn't it great to be alive?' You could hear this 'greeting of gratitude' up and down the corridor every morning, and it gave them an opportunity to start the day on a positive note. When you say something aloud, it has greater power.

A seven-day programme to live from the soul

Actions form habits – talking doesn't. If you want change in your life, take action. Do something. We can take responsibility for making those changes that are necessary to form, and to reinforce, good habits. That's how our virtues are formed. Start small. Change small things in your daily routine. Then watch how, if you really commit to these small changes, other parts of your life will also begin to change in all kinds of positive ways.

This seven-day programme will support you in forming habits which will help you to live from your soul.

Day one

Make the choice to live from your soul

.....

> 'Thou hast made us for Thyself, O Lord,
> and our heart is restless until it finds its
> rest in Thee.'
>
> – St Agustine

.....

St Augustine made this discovery after living a life for many years of wine, women and song. After seeking happiness and satisfaction in external things and other people he finally realised that he was searching in the wrong place. Peace and happiness can only be found deep within your heart and soul. It can only be found in living from your soul.

We have been created as human beings – with a body, mind and soul. Our bodies and minds are limited: they will eventually die. Our souls, though, will live forever. At the level of body and mind we are limited but at soul level we are made in the image and likeness of God and so there is no end to the beauty, the goodness, the giftedness, the love, truth, hope, joy, faith and compassion that is within each of us.

When we choose to live from our souls we bring out what is best in each one of us, and we call forth what is best in each other.

Life, when we live at soul level, is much easier. We are connected with the power of God within. It is like being on the rotary mower rather than trying to cut a meadow with a hedge clippers.

......

Prayer

Jesus, I surrender my life to you.
You take care of everything,
Give me the grace to surrender my life to you.

......

To do today

I'm not asking you to accept what I am saying about living from soul level. I'm asking you to experience it. Make the choice today to be attentive and live from your soul rather than from your mind. During the day, if you find yourself getting angry or annoyed with another person, remember that you have a better place to come from than your head; that deep within you is the power of God himself and that you can call in this power.

We are all human, and none of us is perfect. We all struggle to live from soul level all of the time – I certainly don't succeed. But the more attention we give to living from soul level the easier it becomes.

Be aware that you have a choice to live from the soul. If something goes wrong or you get annoyed remember to go deeper, to go down, away from your head. I find it helpful to use a physical gesture when I find myself acting or speaking from my head. I bring my hands down, fast, from chest to waist level, willing myself out of my head – and this, I find, helps me to remember to act from my soul.

Day two

Acknowledge your own goodness and love yourself

· · · · ·

'"Love your neighbour as yourself." There is no commandment greater than these.'

– Mark 12:31

· · · · ·

If you don't love yourself you can't love your neighbour. Unless you can see your own goodness you are unable to see the goodness in others. So many people I come across have low self-worth, they have missed out on knowing about their own goodness and this has affected their relationships with other people as well.

You are beyond price not because of what you do, but because of who you are: a person made in the image and likeness of God. You are created unique, original and unrepeatable. God created you this way, and he never intended you to be like anyone else.

We need to begin to see ourselves as the beautiful people we are, we need to accept ourselves 'warts and all'. Within each one of us there are positive elements, like buds on a tree, ready to blossom; when we allow ourselves to accept and to love ourselves we allow ourselves to flourish and bloom.

When we love ourselves we are automatically in touch with our inner being, with our soul, which revitalises and energises us and makes us aware of our inner strengths. Coming to accept yourself unconditionally and recognising your own goodness will help you to discover the beauty, the wonder, the peace, goodness and giftedness that lies deep within you.

.....

May all that is unforgiven in you
Be released.

May your fears yield
Their deepest tranquillities.

May all that is unlived in you
Blossom into a future
Graced with love.

– John O'Donohue,
'To Come Home to Yourself';
Benedictus/To Bless the Space between Us

.....

To do today

Just be your beautiful self.

When you find yourself doubting your own beauty and goodness repeat to yourself 'I am good. I was always good. God made me good.'

Day three

Be attentive – in the now!

· · · · ·

'The Precious Present isn't something that someone
gives you. It's a gift that you give yourself ...
The present is simply who I am, just the way
I am, right now. And it is precious.
I am precious. I am the Precious Present.'

– Spencer Johnson, The Precious Present

· · · · ·

The present is the only reality there is. Many of us waste a lot of time and energy as well as creating a lot of anxiety and unnecessary stress worrying about the future. We feel guilt and remorse over our past, while we miss out completely on the only time we can actually live – now.

The present well-lived takes care of every yesterday and every tomorrow. The only time we can be happy is now.

In many situations we cannot give our best if we are not truly present. I remember working in the drug unit in Athy that I always had to make a conscious choice as I crossed the threshold into the unit to leave everything outside and become fully present. No matter what was going on outside there, I could only help those boys if I was truly present. That was the only way I could do my best. There are so many things that we can only do if we are fully present.

The present is always manageable even if we are in pain or in trouble – what makes it hard is if we start thinking it is going to last all night and even longer. I remember being told in the noviceship about the Sacrament of the Present Moment. At the time I didn't really understand what it meant. Today I know that being able to live in the moment is a truly spiritual and sacred experience. It is the key to peace of mind, contentment and happiness, as well as being the only way to live life to the full.

·····

Prayer

*O Jesus, I surrender myself to you,
take care of everything!*

·····

To do today

Whatever you are doing today – cooking, working in the office, waiting for a bus, walking along a road – consciously attend to what you have in hand without allowing your mind to wander to other things. Attentiveness is always at soul level and is always peaceful.

When I am in Cuan Mhuire in Ballycarron, County Tipperary, and am worried about something, or struggling with staying in the present moment, I will walk through the couple of fields to the gate. I'll walk slowly with attention, counting my steps. By the time I get to the gate I'll be well grounded.

Day four

Seeing the goodness in people around you

· · · · ·

Grant me to recognise in others, Lord
God, the radiance of your own face.

– Pierre Teilhard de Chardin, SJ

· · · · ·

102

As a child I thought it was a joke when I heard people say, 'Blessed are those who expect nothing, because they will not be disappointed.' Now I realise how true it is. How many of us wear ourselves out with our expectations of others. None of us is perfect; we all have our own giftedness and our own limitations.

My father used to have a saying: 'To be good is great. To tell others to be good is greater, but it is an awful lot less troublesome.' Many of us are good at seeing the faults in others – there are a few people that I thought if I could change them I could create heaven on earth. As the bible says, when we take the log out of our own eye we no longer see the speck in another person's eyes.

When we see our own unique beauty we are able to see the beauty of others. People have so many different talents; it's not about some being better – it is about everyone's uniqueness.

Prayer

*Lord, inspire me to give of my best and make good use
    of the talents you have given me.*

*Show me how to be positive in attitude, appreciating
    and valuing others, always being ready to encourage and
    give praise.*

*Sometimes I draw conclusions about people in terms of what
    I think is meant by 'success' and 'failure', but the 'failure'
    of one person might count as a great 'success' of someone with
    other talents.*

*Lead me never to judge people but to accept others as they are,
    knowing that it is together, each with our differences, that
    we build up your Kingdom.*

Amen.

To do today

I told you earlier in this book about the 'jugs of positive energy' that we pour over people in their first weeks of being in Cuan Mhuire. We can also send positive energy to people and this is a powerful support in helping us to see the goodness that there is in each and every person.

When you are struggling to see the goodness in another, ask yourself what you are bringing to the encounter. Shake yourself up and dust yourself down and call forth what is best in you so you will be able to see what is best in them.

Day five

Embracing your God-given freedom

•••••

'The secret to happiness is freedom … and the secret to freedom is courage.'

– Thucydides

•••••

I remember, when I was in the noviceship, constantly singing a song about freedom. The only words I can remember now are 'Before I'll be a slave I'll be buried in my grave and go home to my Lord and be free.' No doubt at the time I felt hemmed in. In a way, singing my song was a way of counteracting the rigidity of the life. I saw freedom as something that others could take away from me. As years went by I began to see that it wasn't anyone else or anything outside of me who took away my freedom – it was the patterns I developed as a child that nailed me to the cross. As years go by and I continue to do my inner work I experience more freedom. Today I understand that freedom is to be open to whatever God's plan is for each of us and a letting go of all that comes between us and God's plan.

So many things can get in the way of our freedom: addictions to junk food, alcohol, the Internet, patterns of feeling angry, outraged or hard done by, a desire to control what is going on in our lives or to change those around us. These are all holding us back from our destiny, which is to be free.

We all have the potential to move beyond our limited selves to embrace freedom and know that we are being led by God into new lives.

. . . . .

The Grail prayer

Lord Jesus, I give you my hands to do your work.
I give you my feet to go your way.
I give you my eyes to see as you do.
I give you my tongue to speak your words.
I give you my mind that you may think in me.
I give you my spirit that you may pray in me.
Above all, I give you my heart that you may love in me
  your Father and all mankind.
I give you my whole self that you may grow in me,
  so that it is you, Lord Jesus, who live and work and pray
  in me.

Amen

. . . . .

To do today

Make the choice to be open to God's plan for you today.

When I am struggling with something I say the words, 'Jesus I surrender my life to you. You take care of everything.' I have found myself saying this prayer a lot of times over the last months as I have been struggling with a particular issue. Each time I say it I see the stupidity of not handing it over to God. All I can say is that when I do say this prayer I am heard.

Day six
Reach out a helping hand

· · · · ·

'Do your little bit of good where you are;
it's those little bits of good put together that
overwhelm the world.'

— Archbishop Desmond Tutu

· · · · ·

No matter how tired I am or how much I might want my sleep I always leave my phone on at night. It would be terrible to think of someone desperate, out there at night, without someone to call.

I was never so stuck that some help didn't come to me through the grace of Our Lady. I'm a great believer in the power of prayer and I often think what would it be like to wake up and not know that there is help available to you? What would it be like not to know that Our Lady and God Himself are waiting for you around the next bend? Cuan Mhuire wouldn't be able to carry on without prayer and it wouldn't carry on without the kindness of people – often strangers. Kindness is prayer in action.

• • • • •

Prayer

Be kind and merciful.
Let no one ever come to you without coming away
    better and happier.
Be the living expression of God's kindness in your face,
    kindness in your eyes, kindness in your smile,
    kindness in your warm greeting.

– Mother Teresa

• • • • •

113

To do today

Today choose to be kind. Kindness can take many forms: be patient, remain silent, listen (one of the greatest kindnesses we can show anyone), let go of the harsh word, don't judge.

Be gentle with yourself, and then automatically you will be able to be gentle with others.

Day seven
Giving thanks

•••••

*'If the only prayer you said in your life was
"Thank you" that would suffice.'*

– Meister Eckhart

•••••

Taking things for granted is one of the signs of the times. Everything is expected, little is given. Much wants more. A lack of gratitude creates unhappiness, unrest, disease. When we are ungrateful we have no sense of appreciation: we abuse everything.

Grateful people are happy people:

Grateful to God for the gift of life and our very existence.

Grateful for being made in the image and likeness of God – for the unlimited goodness and giftedness that is within us and that we experience and discover for ourselves as we give it away to others.

Grateful for our families and all who help us in life.

Grateful to each other for the love and fellowship we share.

Grateful for having a roof over our heads

Grateful to all who reach out to us in so many ways and who encourage us on our journey.

Grateful for discovering I am good, I was always good, God made me good.

Grateful for my family and friends.

Grateful for having found Our Lady and the Lord Himself.

Grateful for coming to know the power of the positive.

We each have so much to be grateful for, regardless of what is going on in our lives. When we give thanks for what we have we recognise and appreciate it more.

• • • • •

Prayer

Today I give thanks
For life and love and beauty.
My heart is full of gratitude
For faith, and hope and wholeness.
My life overflows
With abundance and generosity.
Today I give thanks to God Almighty
For the provision of all things good.

– Christine Sine

• • • • •

119

To do today

Think of ten things that you are grateful for right now.
How does your life feel when you are ungrateful and
complaining? How different is it when you feel gratitude?

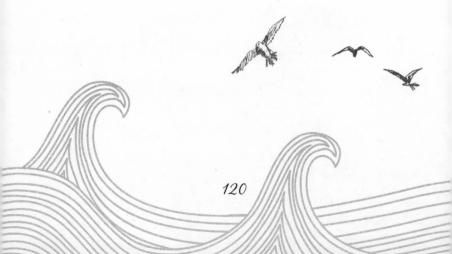

Thoughts from the Old Dairy

At night time in the Old Dairy when all the work was done, we would sit around a small electric fire. We shared our hearts and our worries and our problems. There was so much love and inspiration coming from that group. Everyone went home and brought it with them. The power of love is amazing and God is love, so that explains everything. Love develops. It developed in the Old Dairy and it has a power you can't see but it works all the time.

•••••

I shall pass this way but once: any good that
I can do or any kindness I can show to any
human being, let me do it now.
Let me not defer or neglect it
For I shall not pass this way again.

– Étienne de Grellet

•••••

I saw this inspirational verse in a shop window in
Cork City, just after I began my training in the North
Infirmary. I decided that I would bring it home as a gift
for Christmas to my parents. I had to save up to get it,

as it cost ten shillings – a third of my month's salary. It summed up for me what life is all about.

The Touch of the Master's Hand

'Twas battered and scarred, and the auctioneer
    Thought it scarcely worth his while
To waste much time on the old violin,
    But held it up with a smile.
'What am I bidden, good folks,' he cried,
    'Who'll start the bidding for me?'
'A dollar, a dollar. Then two! Only two?
    Two dollars, and who'll make it three?'
'Three dollars, once; three dollars, twice;
    Going for three …' But no,
From the room, far back, a grey-haired man
    Came forward and picked up the bow;
Then wiping the dust from the old violin,
    And tightening the loosened strings,
He played a melody pure and sweet,
    As a carolling angel sings.

The music ceased, and the auctioneer,
     With a voice that was quiet and low,
Said: 'What am I bid for the old violin?'
     And he held it up with the bow.
'A thousand dollars, and who'll make it two?
     Two thousand! And who'll make it three?
Three thousand, once; three thousand, twice,
     And going and gone,' said he.
The people cheered, but some of them cried,
     'We do not quite understand.
What changed its worth?' Swift came the reply:
     'The touch of the Master's hand.'
And many a man with life out of tune,
     And battered and scarred with sin,
Is auctioned cheap to the thoughtless crowd
     Much like the old violin.
A 'mess of pottage,' a glass of wine,
     A game – and he travels on.

He is 'going' once, and 'going' twice,
   He's 'going' and almost 'gone.'
But the Master comes, and the foolish crowd
   Never can quite understand
The worth of a soul and the change that is wrought
   By the touch of the Master's hand.

– *Myra Brooks Welch*

I see a lot of people in trouble but I also see the work of our Lord every day. The master for me is Our Lord. I've seen people going in to Confession to unload their baggage, and it's wiped for good. This freedom changes them and allows them to get on with living their lives in the present moment and to listen from within. When people deal with their issues, the real person comes out.

· · · · ·

'Consider the lilies of the field, how they
grow: they neither toil nor spin.'

— Matthew 6:28

· · · · ·

My little sister Agnes had Down syndrome. As she got older we began to notice that she could not walk or talk like the rest of us. I was always aware that my mother worried about her. She brought her to doctors and constantly prayed for her. Agnes gave us all, at a very young age, the understanding that there's a lot more to us than what we do or achieve. If it weren't so, how did Agnes have such a place of love and joy in our lives?

. . . . .

*'Coming together is a beginning; keeping
together is progress; working together is success.'*

– Henry Ford

. . . . .

Team work is everything in Cuan Mhuire. We wouldn't have been able to build the first Cuan Mhuire centre in Athy if it weren't for the support of the people from the Old Dairy. When we work as a team, we share a sense of responsibility and this gives us value and a sense of belonging and ownership. It's so important to be a part of something.

If

If you can keep your head when all about you
    Are losing theirs and blaming it on you,
If you can trust yourself when all men doubt you,
    But make allowance for their doubting too;
If you can wait and not be tired by waiting,
    Or being lied about, don't deal in lies,
Or being hated, don't give way to hating,
    And yet don't look too good, nor talk too wise:

If you can dream – and not make dreams your master;
    If you can think – and not make thoughts your aim;
If you can meet with Triumph and Disaster
    And treat those two impostors just the same;
If you can bear to hear the truth you've spoken
    Twisted by knaves to make a trap for fools,
Or watch the things you gave your life to, broken,
    And stoop and build 'em up with worn-out tools:

If you can make one heap of all your winnings
    And risk it on one turn of pitch-and-toss,
And lose, and start again at your beginnings
    And never breathe a word about your loss;
If you can force your heart and nerve and sinew
    To serve your turn long after they are gone,
And so hold on when there is nothing in you
    Except the Will which says to them: 'Hold on!'

If you can talk with crowds and keep your virtue,
    Or walk with Kings – nor lose the common touch,
If neither foes nor loving friends can hurt you,
    If all men count with you, but none too much;
If you can fill the unforgiving minute
    With sixty seconds' worth of distance run,
Yours is the Earth and everything that's in it,
    And – which is more – you'll be a Man, my son!

– *Rudyard Kipling*

This poem is a lesson to us all. We have to go deeper within ourselves. We are all only human.

·····

'I shall spend every moment loving.
One who loves does not notice her trials;
or perhaps more accurately she learns
to love them.'

– St Bernadette Soubarious,
from her private diary

·····

We all have our trials. I, like everyone, have had very tough times in my life. Hard as it may seem, suffering provides us with an opportunity to grow and to love more, if only we are able to learn to accept it.

·····

*'Those who say it cannot be done should
not interrupt those who are doing it.'*

– *Unknown*

·····

I have lost count of the number of times over the
years I have been told that something is impossible,
that it couldn't be done. Yet with the help of God and
Our Blessed Lady it has been done. Cuan Mhuire is a
testament to this.

· · · · ·

*'The highways of the world are covered
with flattened squirrels because they
couldn't make up their mind.'*

· · · · ·

So often in my life I find myself asking 'Am I right? Am I doing the right thing?' There comes a time when the doubting and the talking has to stop. Action creates results and changes things; talking about it doesn't. Sometimes we just need to act.

• • • • •

'Without love, deeds, even the most brilliant, count as nothing.'

– Thérèse de Lisieux

• • • • •

The most important thing in the whole wide world is love.
I first read about St Thérèse when I was eleven or twelve and since then I have had a great devotion to her. I am continually inspired by the beauty and simplicity of her words.

• • • • •

'No one is useless in this world who lightens the burdens of another.'

– Charles Dickens

• • • • •

We all need to be helped. Throughout my life, I have never been stuck, because I always had someone to help me, and I thank God for that always. I leave my phone on at night because I want to be there for anyone who might call in their hour of need. If we can all do that, be there for someone else, they will know that help is available to them, and that will make all the difference.

'To acquire wisdom is to love oneself.'

– Proverbs 19:8

. . . . .

When people come to Cuan Mhuire, we tell them to embrace their own goodness and to stop beating themselves up about the negative aspects of their past and their behaviour. We have to take ourselves as we are at that moment and look forward. There's no life in the negative, and focusing on it can make us lose faith in our own goodness.

Prayers from the Old Dairy

What would it be like to wake up and not know that there was so much help and peace available to you? I don't know what I would do without the power of prayer. The bottom would go out of my world.

Sometimes we think God doesn't hear our prayer – but I believe he does. I know in my heart and soul that I'd be useless without the power of prayer.

God sees the whole picture and he sees into our hearts and what we are letting ourselves in for.

We can't know whether what we are praying for is good or bad for us. If a child kept begging for a shiny, sharp, dangerous knife you'd never give it to them regardless of how often they asked.

We are so short-sighted we can hardly figure out the *now* and very little more. God sees the long-term plan – that's why we need to pray and then trust in God.

Here are some of my favourite prayers. I include a number of prayers to Our Lady as I have been asking for Her help since I was a very young age and I trust I will continue to do so until my dying day. She has always answered my call.

Morning prayer

.....

*Oh my God, I believe so firmly that you
watch over all who hope in you, and that
I can want for nothing when I fully rely on
you for all things. That I am resolved no
longer to have any anxiety, but to cast all
my cares on you.*

.....

I say this prayer before or after meditation every day.

Night prayer

• • • • •

*Oh my God, I believe so firmly that you
watch over all who hope in you, and that
I can want for nothing when I fully rely on
you for all things. That I am resolved no
longer to have any anxiety, but to cast all
my cares on you.*

*In peace and in the same trust, I will sleep
and take my rest, for you, oh God, have
settled me in hope.*

• • • • •

At night I say a similar prayer with an additional prayer
for sleep.

Prayer of surrender

. . . . .

Jesus, I surrender my life to you.
You take care of everything,
Give me the grace to surrender my life to you.

. . . . .

We are not in control of everything, which is important to remember when we have setbacks in life. This is the prayer I say, not just on such occasions, but all the time.

I must say this prayer one hundred times a day. I say it when I'm in trouble. I say it when I want something. I might be shaking in my shoes, or lying awake at night, and I'll be saying this prayer.

Prayer of faith

· · · · ·

Come to us, O Holy Spirit, as you came to the Apostles.
Open our minds that they may be filled with the hidden
*   things of God.*
Send your love into our hearts like a flame of fire
*   that our lives may be changed by your power, O Holy*
*   Spirit, to do God's will on earth and bring others with us*
*   to heaven.*

– Fr Bernard McGuckian SJ

First appeared in *Messenger*, Irish Jesuits, 2007

· · · · ·

I hold great faith in the power of believing, though at times it may be difficult. One day I asked my good friend Father Barney to say a prayer with me. He suggested a prayer that he had learned from his mother when she was in her nineties.

Prayer of gratitude

· · · · ·

Thank you Lord for loving us.
Thank you Lord for taking care of us.
Thank you Lord for everything ...

· · · · ·

I make this prayer up as I go along, thanking the Lord for whatever I have to be grateful for at the time.

The serenity prayer

. . . . .

God, grant me the serenity to accept the things I cannot change,
Courage to change the things I can,
And wisdom to know the difference.

. . . . .

This prayer has the power to help all people. Our defects run so close to our giftedness.

Prayer to the Holy Family

· · · · ·

Jesus, Mary and Joseph,
in you we contemplate
the splendour of true love;
to you we turn with trust.

Holy Family of Nazareth,
grant that our families too
may be places of communion and prayer,
authentic schools of the Gospel
and small domestic churches.

Holy Family of Nazareth,
may families never again experience
violence, rejection and division;

may all who have been hurt or scandalised
find ready comfort and healing.

Holy Family of Nazareth,
make us once more mindful
of the sacredness and inviolability of the family,
and its beauty in God's plan.

Jesus, Mary and Joseph,
graciously hear our prayer.
Amen

•••••

We said this prayer at home all the time when we were younger.

The Rosary

My mother always tried to make life better for people. When anyone was sick in the locality she visited them, maybe staying overnight when a neighbour was very ill. She helped in any way she could. She was always saying prayers for the sick and troubled people she knew, and as children she always reminded us to do the same. Her favourite Novena was the Rosary Novena, which she said all the time, in addition to the Family Rosary. When it came to something particularly difficult, we would say the Novena to St Jude. For us children, this meant walking a return journey of eight miles to confession every second Saturday. We saw it as part of life. It came naturally to us.

We always said the Rosary at night time. No one ever said to us as children that we had to pray – instead we followed our parents' example. The Rosary said when we are little stays with us. I once met a lady after Mass who

was looking after her mother, who was suffering from dementia. The only peace her mother got was when she was saying the Rosary – she'd never forgotten it.

In inviting us to say the Rosary, Our Lady is reaching out to help us. We need to listen. Some may feel that there is no space for family prayer, with TV and music and smart- phones and the like in our way. There is always a space and a time if we make that time. Say it in the kitchen, the heart of the home, and start it early. Children grow to love saying their 'own decade'.

The Rosary covers all the events in the life of our Lady and Her Son – events that are very familiar to many families. You can identify with what Our Lady was going through – Her life events, the sufferings and the joys. Our Blessed Lady's experience of having a child outside of marriage – in a time and a place where you could have been stoned to death for it. Their journey to Bethlehem.

Joseph's disappointment in not getting a safe place for his wife from his own kin. Then, when the Child was born, they had to emigrate in fear of their lives. And how Our Lady felt when She had to search for Her Son for three days. The Rosary carries us through the events of the life of Our Lord.

The Rosary was so important to us in the early days of Cuan Mhuire. It was said at 11 p.m., because that's when the pubs closed so we knew someone was missing if they didn't turn up. There were many times when we would have to go looking for them at 11.30 p.m. or later after the Rosary was said. Prayer brings people together. It nourishes the spiritual dimension that is at the core of our being. Since his death, my brother Johnny's house is now called Rosary House, as every Friday people gather there to pray. When the cars are parked around the house, people know that the Rosary is happening, and our dear friends and neighbours come together. It's a great boon to the community as a shared activity and a bit of peace in our busy week. There isn't one bit of gossip here. We have tea and cake afterwards, and people take it in turns to provide for their friends and neighbours.

The Memorare

· · · · ·

Remember, O most gracious Virgin Mary, that never was it known that anyone who fled to your protection, implored your help, or sought your intercession was left unaided.
Inspired by this confidence, I fly to you, O Virgin of virgins, my mother. To you I come; before you I stand, sinful and sorrowful.
O mother of the Word Incarnate, despise not my petitions, but in your mercy, hear and answer me.

Amen.

· · · · ·

I might be praying words like 'inspired by this confidence' but that doesn't mean I feel that way. My heart might be full of trouble, but as I say this prayer over and over trust grows in me. This prayer has carried me through tough situations.

Totally yours

• • • • •

Immaculate Concept, Mary, My Mother.
Live in me. Act in me. Speak in and through me.
Think your thoughts in my mind. Love, through my heart.
Give me your dispositions and feelings.
Teach, lead and guide me to Jesus.
Correct, enlighten and expand my thoughts and behaviour.
Possess my soul. Take over my entire personality and life.
Replace it with Yourself.
Incline me to constant adoration and thanksgiving.
Pray in me and through me.
Let me live in You and keep me in this union always.

– Maximilian Kolbe

• • • • •

This is a prayer said by Pope John Paul II.

To Our Lady

•••••

Mother of sure hope, in all our moments of doubt and trial, obtain for us the grace to serve your son as you did, with deep faith and calm courage and hearts untroubled by mistrust in Him and in His everlasting love.

•••••

Our Lady had such great faith. If you are ever in doubt ask Her can you borrow Her faith.

Prayer to Mary, Undoer of Knots

·····

Virgin Mary, Mother of fair love, Mother who never refuses to come to the aid of a child in need, Mother whose hands never cease to serve your beloved children because they are moved by the divine love and immense mercy that exists in your heart, cast your compassionate eyes upon me and see the snarl of knots that exist in my life.

You know very well how desperate I am, my pain and how I am bound by these knots.

Mary, Mother to whom God entrusted the undoing of the knots in the lives of His children, I entrust into your hands the ribbon of my life.

No one, not even the evil one himself, can take it away from your precious care. In your hands there is no knot that cannot be undone.

Powerful Mother, by your grace and intercessory power
with Your Son and My Liberator, Jesus, take into your
hands today this knot ... I beg you to undo it for the
glory of God, once for all, You are my hope.
O my Lady, you are the only consolation God gives me, the
fortification of my feeble strength, the enrichment of my
destitution and with Christ the freedom from my chains.
Hear my plea.
Keep me, guide me, protect me, o safe refuge!
Mary, Undoer of Knots, pray for me

Worry is a negative energy. It can soak up all your time. It's a total waste of time because there's nothing positive in it. There's nothing good in it. There is no healing in worry. We have to learn how to hand it over to God. He loves us and we should not be afraid of what is to come. If you find your thoughts returning to the worry, replace it with this prayer. Fill the worrying space in your head with it. Pope Francis finds this prayer helpful in times of worry and stress.

Acknowledgements

I cannot begin to know where to start in thanking all of the people, friends, who have been with me on the journey of Cuan Mhuire throughout the years. None of what we have achieved together would have been possible without your friendship, love and support. There were so many I wouldn't have space to mention them but they know how special their contribution has been to Cuan Mhuire and to all of us. Thank you.

In 2016, we celebrate the fiftieth anniversary of Cuan Mhuire and I began what I feel is my most important work, creating the 'Friends of Cuan Mhuire', and my priority in this special year is that these groups be established in towns and cities across the country in small, modest houses. These will be 'homes' where individuals who have completed their treatment programmes in Cuan Mhuire houses can come together to support each other in maintaining their sobriety and from which they can reach out to others who are worried about their own loved ones and friends who are in active addiction. These will be simple meeting places for a chat and a cup of tea in a warm, welcoming and supportive environment: places where those who need help can receive support and encouragement from the *lived* experience of those who have travelled the same road. Friends of Cuan Mhuire will offer to communities from Donegal to Kerry the 'homeliness', the ethos and the warm welcome that is at the heart of Cuan Mhuire's centres and transition houses. I hope that these houses will be places of faith, hope and love, where, as in all Cuan Mhuire houses, the Rosary will be recited each evening by all who wish to participate.

I would love to see a centre for Friends of Cuan Mhuire in every town in Ireland and I would dearly welcome any, and all, help you can provide in this great work.

Permissions Acknowledgements

The author and publisher would like to thank the following for permission to use material in *The Harbour Within*:

'Blessing: To Come Home to Yourself' from *To Bless the Space Between Us: A Book of Blessings* by John O'Donohue, copyright © 2008 by John O'Donohue. Used by permission of Doubleday, an imprint of the Knopf Doubleday Publishing Group, a division of Penguin Random House LLC. All rights reserved.

'The Touch of the Master's Hand' by Myra Brooks Welch (originally published by Brethren Press)

Excerpts from *The Precious Present* by Spencer Johnson, M.D., copyright © 1984 by Candle Communications Corporation. Used by permission of Doubleday, an imprint of the Knopf Doubleday Publishing Group, a division of Penguin Random House LLC. All rights reserved.

'Today I Give Thanks' © Christine Sine. Used with permission of the author. http://godspace-msa.com/2014/11/27/my-favourite-thanksgiving-prayers/

Prayer used for Prayer of Faith by Fr Bernard McGuckian SJ, which first appeared in *Messenger* Magazine, Irish Jesuits, 2007.

Accounts and memories of Sister Consilio's life, her early life in Kerry and St Vincent's were adapted from *A Haven of Hope: The Life and Work of Sister Consilio* by Nora McNamara. The author and publisher would like to acknowledge the use of this book with thanks.

Cuan Mhuire today

Today, Cuan Mhuire is Ireland's largest provider of residential detoxification and treatment services for those suffering from addiction. Providing a 24/7, 365 day a year service and with all faiths and cultures welcomed and valued, Cuan Mhuire still operates on the principle that there are no hopeless cases.

Treatment capacity

Cuan Mhuire has approximately 600 treatment beds nationwide. Of these 106 are designated for detoxification (both male and female). This is a huge plus because such facilities are uncommon in most treatment centres. The annual number of admissions is approximately 3,000.

Detoxification

Typically, this comprises two weeks' detoxification – in a specialist twenty-four-hour nurse-staffed unit, with the necessary medical support and supervision available.

Treatment

It takes place in a loving, caring, family atmosphere and the programme is based on the philosophy of total abstinence. The programme strives not only to address the addiction but also the underlying cause of the addiction and restore the confidence, self-respect and sense of responsibility of the participants.

The programme includes:

- Detoxification (each centre has a detoxification or assessment unit)
- Individual counselling
- Group therapy
- Meditation and relaxation therapy
- Alternative therapies
- Videos/films/lectures

- Therapeutic activities
- Attendance at AA, NA and GA meetings
- Family days

Family support

Central to the Cuan Mhuire philosophy is a sense of belonging, inclusiveness and recognising the importance of the family. Consequently, every effort is made to support the families of those undertaking the programme. Where possible and appropriate, the participation of family in the healing, recovery and rehabilitation of the person on the programme is encouraged and facilitated. Family Days are provided in each treatment centre.

Aftercare

Aftercare is provided for two years for those in recovery and for their families. Meetings are held weekly in various

centres throughout the country. In addition, aftercare is held monthly in each Cuan Mhuire treatment centre.

Residential transition houses

Many of those availing of addiction treatment in Cuan Mhuire centres have been homeless at the time of admission. They have experienced sleeping rough or living in hostels for years. It can be daunting to return to society on completion of their programme, especially if they lack financial and/or family support.

To meet their needs, Cuan Mhuire established its first transition hHouse at 38–39 Lower Gardiner Street, Dublin in the early 1990s. Since then transition houses have been opened in Limerick, Galway, Dublin and Monaghan. Cuan Mhuire currently caters for close to 100 residents in its transition houses.

The purpose of transition houses is to provide a 'home

from home' within an environment which encourages self-awareness, self-respect, self-esteem and a sense of responsibility. Residents stay in these houses for three to six months, or until they feel ready for independent living.

Friends of Cuan Mhuire

'Friends of Cuan Mhuire' is a new support network being established in towns across Ireland, for people in recovery and their families, where people are helped find their feet in the early, and sometimes difficult, days of recovery.

> *'Somewhere to go, someone to talk to, friends to rely*
> *on and a welcome whenever you call by.'*

Each unit is independent, rooted in its own community, managed by the 'friends' themselves and linked in friendship to the nearest Cuan Mhuire centre.

Funding

Cuan Mhuire is a registered charity. It is funded, firstly, by the provision of services to government and government agencies and, secondly, through contributions from residents, including private health insurance companies.

The reality is that neither the income from government nor from residents covers the economic costs of service provision.

This creates a 'funding gap', both in the capital expenditure and day-to-day spending. To date this has been bridged through voluntary contributions from leading Irish and international business individuals, corporate bodies, friends and relations and from fundraising activities.

Continuing support from Cuan Mhuire's many friends and corporate partners is vital to its work across the island of Ireland. The organisation remains reliant on its loyal volunteers, many of whom have recovered through its programme, to fundraise and sustain its distinctive ethos into the years ahead.

To maintain and grow its services, for those most in need and families struggling through the trial of addiction, Cuan Mhuire looks to its friends and the corporate world, who share their ethos, to work with and alongside them in their mission.

More information on donations and bequests to Cuan Mhuire may be found at www.cuanmhuire.ie or by contacting Teach Mhuire on +353-1-1-8788877.